MW00412139

Download Your Bonus Gifts!

You have taken time out of your busy day and will be rewarded with a FREE gift! I created a simple must-have gift for you located on the front page of our website.

- YOU won't be spammed.
- Your data will not be sold to any 3rd parties.
- This is a valuable report that answers the top 20 questions of passive apartment investing.
- The only exchange is your name and email.
- This FREE report will answer questions and is easily viewable on your smart phone by scanning the following code or viewed by entering ViperVenturesLLC.com into a web browser.

SINGLE SEAT INVESTOR

BUILD PROACTIVE WEALTH™
WITH PASSIVE
APARTMENT INVESTING

DOMINIC "SLICE" TEICH

Published by Viper Ventures Publishing

052020

Cover photo by Tech. Sgt. Joseph Swafford, U.S. Air Force

DISCLAIMER:

This book contains the opinions and ideas of the author. The purpose of this book is to provide you with helpful information about passive apartment investing. Careful attention has been paid to ensure the accuracy of the information, but the author cannot assume responsibility for the validity or consequences of its use. The material in this book is for informational purposes only. As each individual situation is unique, the author disclaims responsibility for any adverse effects that may result from the use or application of the information contained in this book. Any use of the information found in this book is the sole responsibility of the reader.

RAVING FANS

Slice (Dominic Teich) brings actual experience to the table. He provides a tactical plan that will save you time so you can accurately target beyond visual range and WIN—every time. I trust that he is making great decisions with our properties as he provides a very hands-off experience that keeps the passive investor informed and worry-free.

Justin Hicks—F-15E / F-16 Instructor & Airline Pilot

As a longtime investor and real estate wealth manager of 23 years in the Arizona real estate market, I understand firsthand the ups and downs of investing. I also understand the tremendous importance of having a turnkey option to building wealth. Slice has hit it out of the ballpark with this book and his offerings to investors. I just wish I had Slice in my corner when I got started decades ago. I would invest with Slice any day of the week.

Mike Weinstein—Real Estate Wealth Manager www.azrecongroup.com

Thanks Slice, I appreciate it and your nailing this venture. I'm impressed with the business approach you use. It really lets us investors know you are: 1) serious and engaged on a project, 2) very active in the realm with research and communication. Keep it up.

Mike Handy—F-16 Instructor & Airline Pilot

I've been a Realtor and investor for almost two decades and known Dom for several years. This book will give you a no-fluff, to-the-point synopsis of getting started in multifamily investing and get you on your path to making money passively in real estate! After working with Dom on his first four property purchases and watching him grow as an investor, I can honestly say I've never had a client listen as intently and implement so quickly these proven strategies. He learned by DOING, and his work ethic and drive are second to none. If my own family wanted to invest, he's one of the very few I would have 100% confidence in referring them to. He is one of the smartest, results-driven individuals you will ever meet. I'd recommend engaging to see how you can benefit!

Eric Ford—The Ford Team & My Home Group

This short and concise handbook is easily understandable for potential investors who are not familiar with multifamily real estate investing. *Single Seat*

Investor educates and guides you through a lucrative investment option that brings to light the importance of knowing and trusting who is the "hands-on" active team member in the deal that assures your investment has profitable returns. Viper Ventures—thank you for giving forward to help all of our pediatric oncology families through Anna's Foundation. Your generosity helps our cause tremendously.

Joe & Polly Schindler—The Anna Schindler Foundation—AnnaSchindlerFoundation.org

A solid case to encourage investors to pursue passive apartment investing as part of their financial portfolios. This book has a well-argued position that should give confidence even to the first-time apartment investor. Slice uses brute force in his deals, and it is always a crowd pleaser.

Jeff Cohen—Retired F-16 Instructor & Airline Pilot

I'm not worried at all. If Slice was to take my money, I know some unemployed Sicilians who would love to track him down. Nice work man! I'm impressed. Thanks again for the opportunity!

Joe Goldsworthy—A-10 / F-35 Instructor Pilot & Business Owner

As a seasoned real estate wealth manager for 20 years, I immediately gravitated to Slice and his methods for the simple fact that: I know these methods work! The fabric of the real estate industry has never changed as much as it has in the recent years. Dominic's Proactive WEALTH approach is the future of real estate. Whether you are a seasoned investor, a first-time home buyer or a tenant, you are an investor. If you are a tenant, you are simply investing in someone else's real estate portfolio. Which category do you want to be in? The business plan Slice has created allows you to not only be the "seasoned investor" but also to do it in a fashion that doesn't require the painstaking hours required to go at it alone successfully.

Ryan Gerdes—Real Estate Wealth Manager
www.azrecongroup.com

Nicely done and well put together. Thanks for sharing. Onward and forward with more projects!

Mike Calkins—VP & COO of Valley Income
Properties

This book contains all that a reader needs to know. It leads the reader to garner investment in the prospects of unique investing. The book is personal in that it shares the author's life and values.

Tim Teich—VP, Global Solar Energy

Dom's book, *Single Seat Investor*, offers a realistic, step-by-step survival guide for the ever-growing demographic shift towards renting versus owning real estate. You can generate Proactive Wealth by educating yourself with Dom's systematic, hands-on experience and sound principals for investing in apartment buildings.

Anthony Johnson—Real Estate Investor

What an achievement. Great work and I love that you tracked the progress from start to completion to take us on a journey. The videos help me justify future projects! This year of 2020 will be another year of growth for all of us.

Eric Little—VP, CommLoan/Commercial Loan Origination

You are crushing the renovations. Put me down for an equity stake.

Todd White—AV-8B / F-16 Instructor & Airline Pilot

This book is a high-speed, to-the-point, resource that is an excellent addition to any investor's collection.

Gabriel Teich—Owner, Private Tech Solutions LLC

The property looks great. I like the finishes. Nice job! BTW, I really like your property videos. I want to have enough of your mailbox money when I retire to never have to touch my savings.

Brian Wilder—Retired F-16 Instructor Pilot & VP, Lovitt & Touché Commercial Insurance

I would highly recommend this book to family and friends who are looking for a secure way to invest their money. It's informative, easy to read and gives me the confidence that I, too, can invest in real estate.

Brittany Teich

The business plan looks sound, and I'm excited to be in on this—our group is 100% in on the equity stake. Let me know when you send the mailbox money.

Scott Kotowski—F-16 Instructor & Airline Pilot

This book is dedicated to my very first business investor—my wife Danielle. I wouldn't have made the first deal happen without your support... and your U.S. currency.

You invested in me and I am forever thankful.

ACKNOWLEDGEMENTS

A heartfelt thank you is in order for the following individuals who were my early investors who made all the difference in the world to me. Without you, these deals would not have happened.

To my dad, Tim Teich, for spending many Saturdays of my childhood working on rental properties and showing me the ropes while demonstrating an unending work ethic.

To my early investors:

- Danielle Teich
- Mark Warner
- Justin Hicks
- Isla Teich
- Maximilian Teich
- Gabriel Teich
- Brian Wilder
- Jeffrey Cohen
- Andrew & Sunrise Stockman
- Mike and Kelly Handy
- Richard & Theresa Teich
- Todd & Sage White
- Scott & Natalee Kotowski
- Joe & Polly Schindler
- Brenden & Kathy Duddy
- Kevin & Ericka Anderson
- Bob Baker
- Nick & Leah Holmes
- Joe & Val Goldsworthy
- Anna Teich

DID YOU KNOW...

... that 95%+ of the Forbes richest 400 individuals hold their wealth in real estate? I'm not talking about how they obtained wealth; I'm talking about how they hold their wealth. Bricks, sticks, and mortar don't fly away into the wind like a falling stock price can.

You can discover that relatively complex apartment investments are easy to understand, and anyone can do it with a small amount of time invested. You are my #1 priority when you decide to invest in your future wealth. I personally guarantee a fantastic experience that will save you time and energy. My business is built around word-of-mouth referrals, so please pass this book along to someone who might benefit from these fantastic strategies once you are done reading it!

CONTENTS

FOREWORD

When Slice (Dominic Teich) first approached me about investing with him in multi-family properties, I was excited for the opportunity to work with someone I trust in investing in a category I had always been intrigued by but hadn't found the time or energy to jump into previously.

I have been investing in the stock market since I was 18 and consider myself, if nothing else, an interested and educated investor. I've had reasonable success with my investments but always wanted to diversify in a category uncorrelated from the market. After working with Slice now in two successful investments, I know I've made a great choice with my investment and am excited for future growth and opportunities.

Here are some reasons I enjoy this investing experience:

1. I trust him—I know that he is making great decisions with our assets and that he truly cares for the investor. More than that, he truly is passionate about his work, and it drives a dedication to the business that is genuine and unflappable. In real estate, the property is part of the equation to a good investment. However, equally important is the person managing those properties, and in Slice, we have a winner. Finally, he is available. Any question I have is answered immediately and clearly.

2. A great diversification tool—throughout my investment journey, I have become very comfortable in the equities. However, you can never be truly diversified in the market alone. Even when you try and diversify in the markets by owning different sectors or different strategies, the market generally moves together. Therefore, I have found real estate to be a great diversification tool that has different drivers of return than the market.

3. Real estate advantages—beyond helping diversify a portfolio, real-estate returns have tax advantages over equity returns and also provide cash flow. Cash flow is important here. With interest rates at all-time lows, the bond markets don't provide cash flows as they did in the past, and if interest rates

begin to rise, those bond portfolios will decrease in value. The properties Slice has offered have the ability to generate excellent cash flows untethered to interest rate risk while offering tax advantages through depreciation strategies. Bottom line, they are a great tool in any investor's portfolio.

4. Hands off—I'm busy; I have 4 kids, a wife with an excellent engineering career, and two jobs myself. Real estate is a great investment but one that takes a lot of time and personal attention if you want to own properties. Because of this, I've never had the ability to own a property. Slice changed that. He takes the work on and lets you be hands off, while providing plenty of updates throughout the project to know your money is working smartly to earn you a return. Though there are crowd-funding, real-estate platforms out there these days, you don't know who is making the decisions or where the money is actually going. With Slice (reference reason #1), I know who is managing my money and investment, and that makes all the difference in making this work.

5. Reliable returns—every contract I have signed has been honored. Returns have been as promised and on time. There is always risk in any investment, but this has so far been as worry-free of a product as I have found.

Bottom line, I have enjoyed working with Slice and have been thoroughly impressed and pleased with the investments I have made through his business. I am incredibly excited for the future and can't wait to see what other opportunities arise!

Mark Warner

F-16 Instructor & Commercial Airline Pilot

WHO SHOULD READ
THIS BOOK?

So there I was, surveying the landscape out the window of my single-seat fighter jet over the desolate Middle Eastern terrain, the other side of the world. At 25,000 feet in an air-conditioned cockpit, the incredible views of the F-16's bubble canopy casually framed miracles by the minute. It was like clockwork, every 35 minutes my wingman and I would peel away from our assigned tasking to rendez-vous with the air-refueling jet. Only this time, I was visually taking in the war-ravaged countries consumed by terrorists in the fifth month of my second deployment.

As the sun rose over the horizon, the mountains started to jut out and rudely disturb the orderly line of the horizon. Instead of seeing the densely green forests that I saw in the USA, the sand extended as far as the eyes could see outside of the pockets of burning cities that dotted the desolate landscape. The two main rivers that I had read about in the Bible were easily viewed from my altitude: the Tigris and Euphrates. My goal of flying a fighter jet had been one that I achieved and had been working towards the better part of my life. But now, comfortably seated inside my machine, optimally reclined at thirty degrees, oxygen mask down and mustache out, I faced a somewhat difficult dilemma. Even in the midst of what would be a breathtaking spectacle, time froze.

The transit to the tanker brought on thoughts of my wife, daughter, and two-month-old son that had been born during my deployment. How best can I help them with their dreams now that I have achieved mine? And that's when I got my revelation. How could I continue to be a pilot and also start a company that builds Proactive Wealth that lasts for generations?

What Does It Mean to be a Single Seat Investor™?

I'm Dominic Teich, and I help passive investors grow Proactive Wealth and minimize their taxes on cash returns by investing in apartment communities. I decided to write this book because I'm a single-seat fighter pilot and want to show you how to own equity in apartments. This book shows you how to leverage my background in business, real estate, construction, and military training to help you create wealth— proactive and generational wealth that survives the market ups and downs.

I'm talking about wealth that lasts into your later years and that provides comfort, stability, cash flow, tax benefits, and increased time to do what you want to do. It's Proactive Wealth that you can actively build by owning equity in apartment communities.

Why Do We Call It Proactive Wealth?

It takes initiative for a passive investor to review and chose to invest in apartment communities. The proactive part only happens when the passive investor realizes that they can participate in partial ownership of an apartment community without having to manage all day-to-day operations and still receive equity and cash distributions that is even more beneficial than owning the real estate yourself or investing in a real estate investment trust (REIT). It is a very proactive way to grow your wealth because this proven system utilizes industry professionals to run the investment for you.

If I were to pick the optimal Single Seat Investor, the following is a list of who would fit that profile.

They would be a person (an investor) who:

- Fears running out of money before they run out of years to live.
- Knows that the costs of living and health care aren't decreasing and they want something to provide historically-sound cash flow for life.
- Is financially sound with $35,000+ in liquid cash to invest.
- Doesn't have the time to own and operate property themselves.
- Fears potential stock market volatility and wants another vehicle for diversification.
- Wants to add more time back into their lives, not detract from it by adding more projects.
- Is responsive during the closing timeline of property purchases.
- Loves seeing money sent to their bank account without having to actually fix toilets, manage renovations, deal with property managers, or take calls in the middle of the night.
- Realizes that businesses can't be forced into an excel document and that there are always challenges running a project that will be unforeseen but that can be handled.

- Wants to see how apartments equal to 5 units or more have a sustainable and profitable trajectory that is unlike other real estate investment opportunity.

- Wants a proven system that provides a world-class service to run their investment in an actual apartment community, not a blind fund or REIT riddled with fees.

- Refers their friends to us after a successful and profitable interaction so they can also benefit from our services.

I want you to see how putting your money in apartment real estate can make your life easier. This book contains a proven formula. If you are a pilot or working professional who doesn't have time for active real estate ownership but who has available cash to invest and wants to diversify into an asset class that doesn't react to the stock market ups and downs, THEN this is the Charlie in the Chocolate Factory golden-ticket elevator ride.

Most will not fit the profile or be interested in what I have to say in the following pages. Some will be offended—others excited. I want to make it abundantly clear on what you are getting into before spending the next 60 minutes reading what this book is about. I am unapologetically "selling" in this book, not only the concepts of owning equity in apartment communities but also why working directly with me as your guide is a smart and effective way to grow your Proactive Wealth. My 'why' for starting this business started with my personal transformation, but 'why' I do this business is for one reason—*profit*. Maximizing profits and increasing the wealth of my passive investor base is my #1 goal; it's that plain and simple.

If you are one that is even slightly predisposed to investing in real estate for profit, and if you would like to learn how to make passive cash flow that has legal tax benefits to shelter your income, and if you want more freedom in your life to do the things you want, you should read this book.

Dominic "Slice" Teich

MY PROMISE TO YOU

I guarantee, as a Single Seat Investor, you will have a quality investment experience that provides world-class service, informed and honest updates throughout each deal, and a conservative business plan so that we can achieve success on each deal.

The following is a list of the ways you will be educated and benefit from investing an hour to read this book. You will learn:

- The practical skills of passive apartment investing.

- How to take the first step to invest in an apartment community.

- Why REITs aren't going to give you the same wealth accumulation as owning equity in an apartment community.

- How apartments provide consistency that is almost scientific.

- What questions to ask the active partner that runs the deal and how to evaluate them.

- How joining together with other investors allows everyone to purchase a much larger apartment community that minimizes the risk and increases profit.

- What red flags to avoid and tricks that active partners don't want you to know when reviewing prospective business plans.

- How to understand the process from pre-purchase to final sale of the property.

- The biggest and most common underwriting mistakes.

- The typical active partner fees.

- The positive tax implications of owning passive apartment investments.

- How to check alignments of interest in a deal and judge performance.

This book shows you that the complex process of owning apartments is easy as 1, 2, 3. There is an inherent risk in every investment just like there is an inherent risk in walking across the street. You have money right now that is being used inefficiently, is losing its value due to inflation, and has enormous value waiting to be set free.

Contact Me for Your Custom "Mission Planning Session"

I help people passively invest in apartments to grow their Proactive Wealth. Each property may have one investor or many; it really depends on your desired strategy. I want to extend a personal invitation to contact me to start your journey towards passive apartment investing and answer any questions. This process is simple, stress-free, easy and informative. This short phone call will make sure that we are both a good fit for each other.

You won't be spammed, and I won't sell your data or personal information.

This is a personal experience that I don't take lightly—I appreciate and respect your privacy.

Please reach out to me at your earliest convenience at ViperVenturesLLC.com/contact-us.

P.S. Make sure you ask about our exclusive **Single Seat Millionaire Equity Club**.

CHAPTER 1

WHY APARTMENTS?

A Loomis armored truck filled with your money won't be following your hearse to your gravesite. The IRS will gladly spend your money while you are here and after you are gone; beware.

Wealth outside of Wall Street...it's possible.

My mind fogged over like the final approach into Chicago when I realized that I may not ever exit the rat race. My internal struggle stemmed from the fear that even if I climbed the ladder and was the chief pilot of an airline or the CEO of a company, I wasn't going to be able to hand that career to my kids to carry on for generations; I'd retire and move on.

I thought I'd be stuck in the machine that drained me of my time indefinitely. Don't get me wrong; I was happy with my career and family life. Improvements to my high school and college years had increased. In college, I scraped just enough money together each month to pay for gas, lived on $0.89 bean burritos, and never made more than $11,000 in any one year prior to entering the military. I realized that if I was to actually take control over my time, I was going to need to do something much different. I needed to reshape the way I viewed investing.

I began as an investor that could be described as a professional speculator. My grandfather said that people go to Vegas to 'invest' in the casinos. I thought that was a witty play on words as it helped me see that the casinos only work because they win and I loose. This gambling mindset permeates the stock market as most people, including myself, invest in stocks because they believe they can increase their wealth quickly and without labor. This is true during all historic bull markets when the average investor becomes convinced that stock values will rise indefinitely.

After successfully running a business that invests in apartment real estate, I wanted to show you that the road you travel does not have to be bumpy, tense and conflicted like mine was. The business minor that I received from Embry Riddle Aeronautical University didn't prepare me for what it actually takes in the real world. The business classes provided the basics, but applying the knowledge correctly in real life was much different than the classroom.

I've made a lot of mistakes in my businesses of the past—I now consider them an expensive education. By the time I was 26 years old, I had paid off $75,000+ dollars in school debt, traveled the world in the Air Force as a T-38 & F-16 instructor pilot, and owned single family rental homes.

Elimination of college debt facilitated a mindset change after talking with some apartment owners. During our conversation, they told me that I had not created a business but had created another job for myself that took a lot of work and oversight. Managing properties and dealing with tenants took a lot of time and energy. This put me on a journey to read and study any book regarding apartments and investment real estate. After spending two years learning how to underwrite, increase value, and fund apartment communities, I was ready; mind you, this was after owning and renting single family homes for eight years. Success came from reading books on how franchises were owned and operated. Professional systems allowed businesses to profit by having steps and checklists for every aspect—the secret to owning a business and not another job.

On my first apartment purchase, I went all in. I sold a car that I had restored when I was 16 years old, sold some gold and silver, cashed out a retirement account, asked my wife for some of her money, and used some savings. During the renovation process, two pilots invested in the deal and brought it to fruition. It worked. Although a little scary at the outset, I was committed to do whatever it took to succeed. My mentality shifted from interested, to massively committed, to "I have no choice but to succeed." I learned that there are no failures, just outcomes that lead to learning opportunities.

Tony Robbins said that, "The secret to living is giving." Giving time and money to benefit others really accelerated our business plan. My cousin Anna died of liver cancer at the age of 7. Her parents started The Anna Schindler Cancer Foundation, and they support families in Spokane, Washington, during this chaotic, emotional, and life-altering event. They provide homes for families so that they can have a place to escape while navigating the treacherous waters of childhood cancer.

When I made the decision to start investing in their cause, it opened up an entire world. Why not push the limits and fund an entire home for a family? Why not fund an entire apartment complex for needy families? What's stopping us? These ideas made me think much bigger...

Approaching the 10-year mark of daily dedication, I started to see results. After years of scraping, saving and educating myself, I was finally able to see some fruits of my labor. I didn't want to shoot fish in a barrel; I wanted a bazooka and a large fish stuffed in the bottom of a small tuna can so that I couldn't miss! Apartment communities provided a measurable, quantifiable, and tangible asset that helped my investors grow their wealth securely; I was their humble guide.

Here's What You'll Discover

Your job and mine is being reshaped and redesigned. People aren't. The employee union that you think will protect you, won't. With the stroke of the pen and the swift business decision of the man, they will take your job and furlough you.

Money market funds, government bonds, and bank CDs are like a propeller driven cargo aircraft: slow, straight line, and a constant and effective means to an end. The trustworthy propeller-driven cargo aircraft will get you there, but it may take a while.

Apartments are the fighter jets in your portfolio. They race to the target, minimizing location error on your first-run attack. Apartments are about putting your after-tax dollars in an asset class that has legal protections that accelerate your currency back to you—all of it.

The current age and demographic shift is decisively shaping all industries, and more than ever, there is a massive surge of the U.S. population towards renting versus owning a home—both young and old.

A $50,000 investment now at 10% growth for 20 years equates to $336,375. If an additional $10,000 per year is added during that term, that number grows to $966,399.99. That is a 673% increase with a $50,000 investment now and a 1,933% increase by just adding an additional $10,000 every subsequent year. It is not uncommon for apartment communities to meet and exceed these projected returns.

I don't like investing; I like the profits that are made from investing. Those profits add additional fuel to our investors' lives and ours. I have created from-scratch wealth and am deeply committed to that ideal.

Here's Why This Is Different

A few years back, I remodeled an investment property for three weeks during my Christmas break. When I'm lying on my death bed, I guarantee that I won't be thinking about that decision. What I will be grateful for are the profits that were generated from that property and the amount of time that it gave back to me. Passively owning equity in an apartment community is more profitable and less work than owning and renting out your own single-family homes. You do not have to give the same amount of personal effort by utilizing this investment strategy. You are buying wealth and more time for your career, family and/or other life events. The strategies outlined herein aren't 'perfect' strategies but, rather, strategies that are consistently perfected.

Do you have a plan that generates historically Proactive Wealth that can absorb the shock to your portfolio if other assets crash?

Why This Is Important to You Now

Why would the wealthiest individuals on our planet choose to put their capital in this investment vehicle? The historical proof is that apartments increase wealth. This stuff isn't rocket surgery; if only slightly average humanoids like myself have a shot at this, you can too. Heck, this stuff isn't even near as cosmic as flying a small civilian aircraft for the first time. Our proven system makes it easy for you to educate yourself and avoid missteps along the way.

If you are wary of others taking your money and investing it, you aren't alone. With all the stock market turmoil, the international pandemics occurring every 10 years, and toxic political landscape, you have become a natural doubter and rightfully so. You can answer the questions to those deep-seated fears in this book.

The "American Dream," the idea of owning a

home, is DEAD to much of the current U.S. population. Capitalize now on the increased demand by millennials, boomers, and seniors for apartments; the demographic shift is in full-force.

CHAPTER 2

TIME-SENSITIVE TARGETING FOR PROACTIVE W.E.A.L.T.H.™

I grew up traveling and playing music with my family. During our trips, I completed in many bluegrass fiddle competitions and won prizes and cash. Our band was also hired to play at venues for hotels, business parties, and events. The music competitions did not provide a reliable stream of cash because I didn't always win. The revenue generated by performing in venues provided income, but we had to keep performing in events to make money. And it turned into a job.

None of these things generated lasting wealth because if we stopped playing music, the money stopped coming in. Apartment communities generate Proactive Wealth that don't require constant work.

W—Wealth

Wealth is a product of carefully fashioned systems that generate constant streams of cash flow while increasing equity. The richest people on the Forbes 400 list hold their wealth in real estate. I used the word 'hold' intentionally because I am not stating that they 'made' their money in real estate. Nobody is going to tell you that because it doesn't make them money in fees from your 401k, REIT, or tax imposed by the IRS.

Where does the cash flow come from in an apartment investment?

- Rent
- Fees for storage
- Billing back the utilities to the residents
- Pet fees
- Coin-operated laundry
- *Other fees...(if it's on the lease, it's a legally binding form of cash flow)

There are 3 ways to build Proactive Wealth in apartments:

1—Heavy value-add (my personal favorite). Requires the entire property to be renovated and stabilized; these usually take 1–2 years prior to making any consistent cash flow. These deals can be riskier, but with the correct general contractor, property manager, and oversight from the active partner, the upside to the deal can be very beneficial. Generally, these projects are completely vacant or require a complete turnover of the current residents. They require significant capital upfront but have potential for a large payday once the property is stabilized and long-term financing is obtained post-renovation. Most would consider this the riskiest investment as there is no cash flow while the project is underway. This risk is mitigated by having sound underwriting, capital to cover the renovations, and a mortgage broker that can place the correct mortgage on the property once renovations and leasing are complete. Banks consider apartments stabilized with greater than 85% occupancy.

2—Light value-add deal (these deals are competitive). One that has an upside in rents collected, could benefit from installing interior washer/dryers, updating the curb appeal, painting the exterior, doing some touch up jobs around the property, and/or installing one-time capital expenditures that don't have recurring costs associated with them or are offset by increased rents collected. The key here is that the value added to the property is done while there are residents living on-site. These properties are a favorite of active investors as they don't have a ton of heavy lifting; the downside is that the market can be very competitive for these deals.

3—Turn-key property. A property that is already stabilized, the rents are at or near the top of the market, all the renovations complete, and cash-flow is immediate. These properties generally do not provide the highest rates of return, but if purchased at the right price, they can be a solid and consistent addition to your portfolio. With the correct management team in place, these deals provide returns in less than 6 months of ownership.

RESOURCE

If you want to calculate your NET worth—just head to:

www.ViperVenturesLLC.com/resources

and download the "Wealth Tracker." (A complimentary gift I have set up to track your net worth.)

E—Equity

Owning equity, even a portion of a large property, provides tangible wealth to your portfolio. Equity in apartments allows investors to be a legal insider as they get access to the financial statements. Apartment communities are valued differently than properties with less than 5 units; their value can be accurately measured. Increased rent or fees collected on these properties drives the valuation higher, and therefore, makes the equity stake you have in a deal worth more. Couple these factors with job growth, in-migration, and an up-and-coming area, and you are in for a great treat.

Real estate is an illiquid asset; you can't buy and sell real estate like trading stocks in your investor profile online. When you purchase a share of stock, you get one share. Like stock, a real estate investment trust (REIT) is a company that owns, operates, or finances income-producing properties but offers little in the way of wealth accumulation because they are publicly traded like stocks. REITs are more liquid than an apartment community, but they are taxed as regular income and have high management and transaction fees that eat into your profits.

When you purchase apartments at the correct price, you pay for equity at a fixed cost but own the equivalent of much more. For instance, a $50,000 investment in a 20-unit apartment community may buy 5%–10% of the entire community in equity. That equity is yours as long as there aren't stipulations in the legal documents that allow the active partner to push you out of the deal or cut your equity shares. Viper Ventures LLC does not decrease your equity when you buy into a deal, during the ownership, or final disposition. This is an important distinction as the money collected from rental income, refinancing, or sale of the property can be distributed according to your equity percentage owned.

A—Appreciation

I grew up contributing to my dad's real estate deals. The largest paycheck I ever earned prior to 12 years old was a $20 bill after working an entire day installing windows on a rental home. What I came to realize was that Dad forced the appreciation of his properties through renovations. He bought properties that needed repair, fixed them up, rented them out, and created additional wealth by increasing the appraised value of the property. I gained on-the-job knowledge and experience through this process and apply what I learned to every one of our deals.

Beware of the active partner that tries to sell you a deal with capital appreciation factored into the financial projections; this could negatively impact your ability to methodically grow the value of your investment. I won't say never, but I would say that you should NEVER calculate a nebulous metric that counts on capital appreciation. This is called gambling and is not investing. There are neighborhoods that do command a higher sales price, and if you can find deals in an area that have much higher comparable prices than what you pay, there is built-in equity in the deal at purchase. Value-add properties allow forced appreciation through better property management, property upkeep, renovations, and/or amenities that generate increased rental income.

Capital appreciation, i.e., appreciation that happens because the entire neighborhood goes up in value, should only be an added benefit of investing. If investing in properties on the fringe of growth, there are high possibilities that the property will go up in value. This is only one of many investment strategies. Properties that are in rougher areas might generate more cash flow if run correctly, but due to the zip code that they are in, the bankers might not 'see' the same value on paper, thereby affecting long-term financing.

Real estate is very 'local.' Area values can change rapidly from block to block. A neighborhood can quickly go from gated, to blue collar, to decent apartments, to ghetto, to nomadic sheep and goat herders that pillage your property in the middle of the night.

L—Leverage

My uncles that I worked with in construction projects taught me the value of leverage—how to leverage other people's time to grow faster and accelerate a project towards the finish line. Using other people's time, money, and resources is how we leverage our business plan.

The biggest value of leverage is added time. Negotiating during purchase significantly helps leverage the value of the investment by purchasing the property at a deal price, paying full-price and realizing that you can raise rents to increase the value, adding amenities to the property that drive the value up through forced appreciation, and using some good ole' crafty thinking to see another side of the property that the current ownership is missing.

Example: we purchased an off-market property for the seller's asking price—at the time, it was $87,500 per unit. The cheapest comparable property in the neighborhood started at $112,500 per unit. During the time we had the property under contract, the property right behind ours sold for $187,000 per unit, albeit it was in nicer condition.

Our value was leveraged through seeing what the current ownership wasn't. Rent collections were $200 less than everyone else was charging in the area. The property needed an updated curb appeal, and one unit needed a full renovation. And we were going to add interior washer/dryer units to all the units.

Once the curb appeal was finished and the remodel complete, we raised rent immediately from $850 per month to $1,399 per month. That is what I call LEVERAGE! We also leveraged a professional contracting team to run the project and had better-than-average finishing times even though we were in the middle of a global pandemic.

Once the property was stabilized and rents increased, we leveraged our financial position on the project through a refinance and conservatively recaptured some of our project costs by pulling out tax-free dollars to return to our investors.

T—Taxes

I'm not a licensed CPA or a tax attorney. Tax professionals exist on my Power Team described later in this book.

Note: You can invest using an IRA or 401(k) account and receive cash distributions sent directly to your IRA account tax deferred! Please go to Appendix A in this book for the simple steps to make this happen.

When I picked up my girlfriend, now wife, from the airport, I got so excited to see her that I rushed up to her, gave her a big hug, and then head-butted her when trying to give her a kiss; super-smooth move. The lesson here is not to rush a good thing. Tax planning, albeit one of the most boring tasks, pays big dividends at the end of the year and through the lifetime of the investment and shouldn't be rushed!

The Federal Reserve is watering down your purchasing power very quickly. Your job is to figure out how to outpace the way that the blockheads running our bloated government are wasting your currency. God forbid that they are able to swipe your after-tax dollars for another round of bloated government programs. You have the ability to move your money, whenever and wherever you please, on a moment's notice; the power to do this will only increase in the 21ST century due to technology.

The positive tax implications of owning equity in an apartment complex is one of the most beneficial ways to protect your earnings from rental income. Properties that are equal to or greater than five units are considered commercial real estate and are taxed differently than other asset classes. Tax benefits of commercial real estate investments many times offsets the advantages of other investments. Partners that own equity in a real estate deal can capitalize on the legal tax strategies to shelter rental income.

Example: $5,000 fewer dollars in tax each year equates to millions of dollars in wealth. If $5,000 is reinvested at an average of 10% for 40 years, you'd have an additional $2,660,555 in retirement.

The IRS allows you to shelter the income from apartments in the following ways:

1) Deductions

2) Property depreciation (IRS classification of items at the apartment community)

3) Depreciation recapture (a gain from the sale of depreciable capital property reported as income)

4) Accelerated cost segregation (this requires a CPA that is savvy with this strategy)

5) Mortgage interest payments

6) Interest paid on additional loans that were used to improve the property

7) One-time capital expenditures "CapEx" (not an ongoing expense)

8) 1031 tax deferred property exchange

9) Capital gains (when sold, capital gains taxes are imposed by the IRS depending on the amount of money gained from the sale)

    a. Usually this is 0%–20%

    b. *There are no capital gains taxes imposed after a refinance

When selling stock, there will be taxes on the gains. In apartment real estate, there are legal ways to protect earnings. If taxed 20% on a stock sale, that could equate to many thousands of potential dollars forfeited. In real estate, a refinance on a property is not viewed as a taxable event, as the IRS views the refinancing dollars as 'your money.'

As an example, a working professional that makes a salary of $350,000 per year contributes to the IRS in the following way:

- Adjusted Federal Income Tax $92,955

- Social Security $8,239

- Medicare $5,075
- State tax $32,276
- Total tax $138,545
- After tax Salary **$211,455**

Example: If you took the total tax of $138,545 from this example and invested it one time without adding any other contributions and it grew at a 10% rate for 40 years, you'd have an additional $6,270,443.56 in retirement.

Much, if not all, of the cash flow that is generated by apartments is sheltered by paper losses. Net losses are a way to show the IRS that your property does not need to pay taxes and the rental income isn't forfeited to the IRS. A 10% return on your real estate investment may take a 12% return or higher in the stock market after paying capital gains tax.

I can show you how to legally reduce your taxes at no cost to you, increase your income, and associate with others doing the same thing. The IRS does not want you know how much your tax liability is working against your ability to generate Proactive Wealth. Bottom line: maximize your profits with minimum tax through passive apartment investing.

H—Historical Trends

My brothers and I had BB gun fights growing up and chose not to wear eye, ear, or face protection.

The decision to shoot our guns at each other resulted in Dad taking our guns away from us for six months. We learned a historically significant lesson; shooting each other is a bad idea and results in gun confiscation. In addition to our punishment, this earned us more time working on Saturday with Dad on rental properties instead of playing with our neighborhood friends and demonstrated another historically significant lesson to us; his property was generating historically profitable returns.

I have very thoughtfully and intentionally chosen to do an out-of-category business that accelerates investment dollars back to you. This undertaking is in apartment communities because it has a high barrier to entry, is difficult to get started, and is even more difficult to manage the larger it gets if the correct processes aren't in place.

I have chosen to do what most won't. I am obsessed and committed to this business and doing things that I'd rather not do in order to get future results. I have personally picked up needles and condoms, seen my apartment units burned and had properties vandalized, been indirectly robbed by property managers, directly robbed by contractors, had windows broken, rents not paid, drug lords evicted, communities changed, properties gentrified, dumpsters burned to the ground, contractors fired, and termites steal from me on at least one of my properties each month. Those incidents pale in comparison to my drive to return invested dollars back to the real heroes: the passive apartment investors.

Unlike stocks, REITs, and 401ks, real estate is an asset that you can control. Historically, property values trend upward at a fairly consistent rate; even if there is a market crash, real estate values eventually climb back up and continue an upward trajectory. The goal is to find real estate submarkets that are ripe for upgrades and are on the edge of growth. The word "gentrification" means that an area is being upgraded, renovated and more conforming to middle-class tastes. Gentrifying markets are very local compared to the broader 'market' that is experiencing certain trends either up or down. Real estate is like watching grass grow; it's consistent growth can be beautiful to behold if fertilized, cut, and watched carefully.

If you don't hold equity in the deal, you won't get to write off your passive returns, and you will pay taxes on your cash returns. Equity is important because that leads to Proactive Wealth—your WEALTH.

CHAPTER 3

A NONTRADITIONAL MEANS TO AN END

On the night of September 11, my wingman and I were topping off with gas and getting ready to head back and support ground troops over an oil refinery that had been overrun with terrorists. While enjoying the quiet serenity, the distant city lights, the burning oil wells, the random muzzle flash from ground troops, and the security of knowing that I was going to have enough gas to continue, we received a call that we were needed at a location further south—immediately.

On the way to our tasking, we were told that the ground commander needed air support to finish the operation. We were tasked this mission because the command and control agency at the time knew that the A-10 Warthogs in our vicinity over the oil refinery wouldn't make the trip fast enough to get bombs on target. Successful people move quickly, methodically, and have a very persistent way about them. That is the reason I chose to fly the F-16 over cargo airplanes, helicopters, or the A-10 Warthog. All of these platforms have a dedicated and important mission; but I like to move fast!

Just like the airplanes above, you get to choose what mode of transportation you want to get you to the target and back safely. Wall Street, 401k plans, REITs and stocks work for many investors, but what the advisors of these plans won't tell you is that there are options to invest in apartment communities that hold equity. I'm talking about real estate that is deal specific—a plan that is crafted for a specific property that you put your hard-earned money into.

What most do not realize is that an extra $5,000 in tax each year translates to millions in lost future potential net worth. The IRS, REIT trust managers, 401k managers, and stock traders, have $0.00 of financial incentive to show you this figure. In a previous chapter, I outlined how saving $5,000 per year can translate to an additional $2,660,555 million dollars of net worth, just by not paying tax and averaging a 10% return over 40 years. When you invest an additional $5,000 each year on top of the $5,000 you keep, that number grows to $4,868,518.11 at the end of the same 40-year timeframe.

If operated, maintained, marketed, and diligently managed, apartments communities can meet and exceed these numbers.

FALSE BELIEF

I'm about to tell you a true story. If you believe me, you will be well rewarded. If you don't believe me, I'll make it worth your while to change your mind. Let me explain. On March 22, 2019, my good friend Eric called me and was excited about a property that was in close vicinity to Grand Canyon University in Phoenix, Arizona. "It's so incredible," he said, "when you see this place, you won't believe it."

"What will I see?" I ask. "What could be so incredible?"

Eric continued, "When you get down here and see this place, your opportunities will be vastly improved. Your life will be more defined, and everything will make more sense. This isn't just my imagination. I want you to see this place for yourself!"

BACKSTORY

When I looked at the property on Google Earth, I couldn't believe my eyes. I kept driving the streets in the neighborhood to see if what I was seeing was indeed actually what my imagination was telling me or if it was playing tricks on me. My clarity improved. My resolve improved. My commitment massively improved. It was obvious. I kept looking but finding the same results, and I compared the property to what I already owned and for what lay ahead in the next 12 months.

Nothing compared to what I had seen up to this point. I was impressed, shocked, excited, and a little apprehensive, but I just knew that I had to do it. Everything started to come into focus. What did this property do that made my resolve and life so much better? I found out in the coming months, and it has changed my life forever. It can change yours too.

We affectionately named this property "The Pierson Projects." You've often heard that properties and tenants can give you a rash of bad news, but what if you purchased a completely abandoned property that was being used for dangerous and illegal activities? Apparently, the entire neighborhood had seen this property fall into the wrong hands. This property was an eyesore of the community and was considered a rather depressing representation of what could be platinum living.

DESIRE & DANGEROUS COLLEGE DEBT

To start, I began a journey just three months prior looking for a property for college students to live in without having to pay the prices of on-campus living. Students at Grand Canyon University, including my brother, were subjected to restrictive guidelines and given a modest room with shared community space for the back stabbing price of $918 per month. In addition to the very average living that $918 purchased every month, the students were forced to move out two times a year during Christmas and the summer break. Disturbing the college student's schedule two times per year during their studies kept their lives in constant flux and made it rather difficult for them to hold down a job. This disturbs me for several reasons.

The **first reason** is that college debt is the worst possible debt that you can have. It is recourse financing that isn't forgivable, does not let the person declare bankruptcy, and is a soul-crushing mechanism to keep our misguided youth in debt forever.

By 'insisting' that the college students stay on campus at Grand Canyon University, the college's financial coffers were being filled with money for years to come. Colleges have zero incentive to educate students on the financial implications that potentially take decades to pay off. Using simple math, a student's college debt would be increased by $44,064 dollars upon graduation by living on campus at Grand Canyon University, assuming that the cost to rent a room did not increase. This doesn't take into account any interest payments, fees, required food tickets, or any other processes that the banks or college impose on a student while in attendance.

The compounding effect of the interest payments incurred just from room and board would be in excess of $100,000 by the time the student was able to pay off the principle balance. This does not factor in what would happen if those funds were reinvested for the 10+ year timeline that was used to pay the debt off. Ultimately, this could easily equate to $250,000 in net worth per student for room and board if all the ancillary costs were taken into consideration!

The **second reason** this property was the right choice is even more impressive. Our pliable and misguided youth exit high school with a below average sense of what our U.S. currency means. Not only do high schools and educational systems fail miserably in teaching the basics of our legal, political, and monetary system, they also fail at teaching essential life basics that are necessary to generate a future that is unencumbered by the crushing load of unforgivable college debt.

When I graduated from college, I had $75,000+ in school debt, and it took me the better part of 10 years to pay that debt off. Just one day after graduation, my interest rate went from 3.2% to 12.4%. Thanks for the help Wells Fargo. Can I say that getting into debt was a bad decision? I'm not going to say that, but I am trying to prove a point that we, if I, could help at least a small portion of college students, I was going to do it.

YOU CAN BE PART OF THE SOLUTION

Finally, by eliminating the ability to control the students' lives on a daily basis, these students prospered and held jobs in the local community. This was a massive hill for them to climb because for the first two years of school, they were handed, spoon fed, and deceived about what they were actually paying for in their on-campus lives.

You see, this property holds so much more significance than just a roof that shelters residents that are capitalizing on luxury finishes and well-above-average ownership. The entire neighborhood has been completely turned around and is a better place. There are now children riding their bicycles where there once was a dangerous breeding ground for drug addicts and prostitutes. Students' lives are being changed for the better. This property has allowed us to help college students, the community, and children—*our heroic investors reaped the rewards!*

THE POINT OF NO RETURN

I was often asked as the project moved along if I was "crazy" and if this was actually going to work. These negative questions were easily dismissed as the reason I was proceeding with such vigor was more than just renovating a property for profit. The financial benefits that this project guaranteed to everyone was not seen by the fools that didn't take action soon enough. If I have learned anything though this project, it is that I have been able to train my eyes to see what others could not or would not. My investors saw the inspiration in me, and they made the right choice!

Be NOT misled; this property is not a shortcut that will catapult you into the ranks of the less than 1% of the world's wealthy population. With that being said, know that we did not take any shortcuts renovating this property. The weakest link in the operation was the inability of others to visualize the finished product.

With this new opportunity, I was able to see inside myself and find the weakest link. The <u>weakest link in all apartment syndications is the active partner.</u> To combat these known issues, I built a power team, explained in Chapter 6, that minimizes unforeseen downsides to owning multifamily properties. Because of this team, investors tapped into a completely flexible operation that does not have a single breaking point, thereby reducing the risk of the investment.

DRAMATIC DIFFERENCE

You, the educated passive investor, are our #1 priority; we operate on a "keep you happy" concept. So, why should you care? In addition to this deal, I also have many other exciting opportunities that are being shaped right now.

By partaking as a passive investor in one of our cash-flowing properties, you are immediately obtaining access to our exclusive list of investors that get to see our other deals first; this happens before we offer it to other potential investors.

LITTLE SECRETS

The majority of the Forbes top 400 hold their wealth in real estate? In truth, some have actively invested; others own companies that own the land their stores or warehouses occupy. And virtually all have stock in their portfolios or family trusts in companies that, one way or another, own real estate. Consider apartments as the initial doctor visit that prescribes just the right amount of financial ingenuity that will change your life. Far be it from me to make that statement...I didn't have to; it WILL change you.

ANOTHER SECRET

Like you, I really don't want any more disappointment in my life. My business policy is not to disappoint. There are many reasons why YOU will NOT ever be disappointed with the service that my business provides. There are some reasons why THIS WILL BE DIFFERENT. Let me simply give you my word of honor on this. As soon as you become a world-class passive investor of ours in a deal, you have direct access to me via my personal cell phone number. If, at any time, you honestly feel you have not bought a product that is living up to the standard of excellence that I demand, I want you to call me personally, directly. I will personally make it right. If something's wrong that can be fixed, I will jump in and get it fixed. If, for whatever reason, you can't be satisfied, I will personally coordinate a plan to make it right. For once, what is promised, will be.

MAGIC TRANSFORMATION

Candidly, the field of investments is riddled with swindlers. They sell a lot of elaborate stuff and may even promise a backseat ride in a fighter jet—and they love talking about visitor counts and numbers of "friends" and clicks on their websites. They do everything but compare their dollars spent to how many dollars they return. They do anything but deliver the actual promised return.

But "where's the money?" Well in this case, I don't run this business with the sole purpose of making money for *myself*. This is what changed everything. This is my massive transformation that I have been describing. Years ago, I purchased rental properties with my only focus on money for myself. This was the wrong approach, and I struggled for years trying to make sense of why it didn't work well. So, let me tell you. Our 'why' shifted from us to making life easier for other investors and the Anna Schindler Cancer Foundation. My major setback all these years was me.

This company has grown in direct correlation to what we are able to offer you and others—our ability to serve you. A year ago, my wife and I committed to a goal of funding a home for the Anna Schindler Cancer Foundation in Spokane, Washington. These homes give families a place to rest and be with each other when their children are going through cancer treatments.

These projects, these properties, will fund this dream someday. That day will come. It will take time, but I am confident that this will happen one day.

"The Pierson Projects" by the Numbers:

- Purchase price $478,000
- Renovation cost $365,000
- After renovation value $1,046,696
- Money invested $843,000
- **Forced appreciation $203,696 (Money investors created = WEALTH)**

- 10-year cash-on-cash return 11.09%

- 10-year internal rate of return (IRR) 14.88%

What was the value of a $50,000 initial investment once renovations were complete in nine months? $65,281.02 (That's a 30.56% increase in value of investment in less than one year and this does NOT include cash distributions.)

There are many different strategies that increase revenues and returns. In the previous case, the seller of the property wanted to sell quickly, so we purchased in three hours at a bargain price and forced the appreciation through a massive renovation. Sometimes, all a property needs is new management and increased rent!

CHAPTER 4

TACTICAL PLANNING PROCESS—WORK TARGET BACKWARDS

During my mission commander upgrade in the F-16, I learned an inordinate amount of information in less than a two-day timeline. Not surprisingly, this upgrade was performed at a very average level on my part, but I am glad to have gone through the process. The item that kept me on track was a checklist that has helped me in more walks of life than I could have imagined, and I apply it to our deals that we purchase so that I get the most amount of information in the shortest amount of time. This process can help you too.

Before Starting Out, Ask Yourself These Questions:

- What is important to you as a passive investor?

- What information do you need to gain for enough knowledge to take the next step?

- Do you have a system to get you to the level of understanding required?

- What result do you want to achieve once you have taken the steps, and how do you know it worked?

- What type of property do you want to invest in? In Chapter 2, I outlined the different types of properties: heavy value-add, light value-add, and turn-key. Each property has a different strategy that produces different results.

- Are you in need of immediate cash flow, or can you wait 12–18 months for a property to be renovated and stabilized with income-producing tenants?

How a Passive Investor Participates in 3 Simple Phases:

Phase 1—Before Ownership

- Schedule a Mission Planning Session with me to discuss your requests.

- Compile our data and look for a deal that 'fits' your investment requirements.

- Review the business plan once we get a property under contract.

- Review and sign the operating agreement and legal paperwork.

- Transfer the funds into the operating account for the deal.

Phase 2—Ownership

- Receive monthly and quarterly updates on your investment.

- Review quarterly financial documents.

- Provide banking information for direct deposits.

- Receive income from rent collections and refinancing proceeds.

- Use the K-1 investor tax statement to file yearly taxes.

- Call or email active partner for any questions.

- Purchase more equity if another partner wants to cash out of the deal.

Phase 3—Disposition and Sale of the Subject Property

- All partners agree to sell for profit.

- Active partner uses the Power Team to list and get the property under contract.

- Active partner facilitates the closing process.

- Partners sign legal documents to sell the property.

- All partners receive distributions from sale based on equity owned.

- All partners file capital gains tax unless the property was a 1031 exchange.

If you have already read enough and want to schedule a custom Mission Planning Session with me to discuss your investment questions, please reach out to me at your earliest convenience by visiting my site at ViperVenturesLLC.com/contact-us.

If you are a do-it-yourselfer or you want to know a little more about the process that I use when I look at properties for purchase, please go to the following website and download a completely FREE guide labeled, "Proactive Property Purchasing Guide" at ViperVenturesLLC.com/resources.

A methodical process guarantees Proactive Wealth.

CHAPTER #5

THE POWER TEAM

Who are you going to call if the project isn't on track? What are you going to do if something unforeseen happens? Who is on the team that can leverage the right results?

Ray Kroc, the owner of McDonald's, built a franchise prototype that is still very successful because it allows owners a way to implement proven systems that generate consistent profits. These systems revolve around the business, system, and franchisor. Systems are necessary because they lead to order and predictability. Because they are so successful, a franchise provides a proprietary model that is easily implemented to generate uniform predictability. They allow the franchisor to work on the business and not in the business.

Passive apartment ownership allows you to tap into a franchise-style business where the active partner is the franchisor. The added benefit is that passive investors purchase a system that is already in place and that is run by a power team without having to run the deal themselves. This proprietary business is a system that is replicated each time another property is acquired. This orchestrated process moves us from offer, contract, ownership, operations, and disposition.

No plan has all the answers. Nobody can highlight every risk. One person cannot know every conceivable course of action; hence the power team.

The POWER TEAM in apartment ownership provides franchise style predictability.

Members on the POWER TEAM:

- The heroes—passive investors
- The guide—active partner/managing member
- Property managers
- Accountant (CPA) & bookkeeper
- Real estate, securities, and business attorneys
- Mortgage broker, banks and insurance broker
- Title agency
- General contracting team/handyman
- Property broker/real estate agent/direct marketing team

The Heroes—Passive Investors

As a passive investor, the greatest challenge will be the first deal. The most work that you should do at any point in the process is reviewing the business plan that is sent to you prior to purchase as well as the legal documents. There are several time-sensitive deadlines that lead up to the closing of a deal. Prior to closing, it is important to operate with a sense of urgency as there will be a non-refundable earnest money deposit that is forfeited if timelines are broken. Keep the active partner updated when sending money so that documentation can be recorded once received. Due to the massive increase in fraud, it is highly recommended to verify the bank transfer information via an additional source prior to wiring money into the operating account; a simple phone call or text can be an additional way to verify that the information you have is accurate. If wire transfers don't work for you, a physical check sent expeditiously is also a valid form of payment.

Once the deal closes, the active partner should provide quarterly updates and financial documentation at a minimum. This is a general guideline as each deal is so unique, and there may be nothing to report for one property and many updates on another. As a general rule, expect more information if the property is undergoing a renovation and less information if the property is stabilized with tenants paying rent.

The Guide—Active Partner (the person running the processes, deal, and systems)

During our first apartment renovation, there were several people on our power team that were hindering our accelerated growth. After we replaced the general contractor, our renovations were completed six months ahead of schedule, and our tax liability was significantly reduced with a new CPA that was familiar with advanced tax strategies and how they pertain to apartment communities and commercial real estate.

The active partner can be the weakest link if they don't have a power team assembled to manage the transaction from finding, underwriting, funding, closing, renovating, managing, and operating the property until final disposition. The active partner's roles and responsibilities are outlined in the operating agreement for each deal. Clear expectations will directly influence all the relationships that work on a daily basis to increase the amount of money going into your pocket.

Ask the active partner these questions prior to investing:

- Can I run a background check on you?

- How are you adding value or hedging against valuation reductions and rent reductions?

- How frequently do you communicate with your investor base?

- What is your financial review process for a property?

- What is the "worst-case" scenario on a deal, and what do you have in place to avoid this?

- Do you have investor references for your current and past deals?

- Are the projected returns what I would expect to get as an investor, or are there active partner fees that aren't shown?

- How much cash reserves do you keep for each deal?

- How much does the active partner invest?

- Who is managing the property, and how long have you done business with them?

- Have any of your deals gone sideways? If so, did you change your strategy?

Property Manager

The property manager will be responsible for executing the directions from the active partner and will impact the money you get to keep at the end of the year. Due to the increase in digital platforms, many management companies are much more than rent collectors. A larger complex, may support an onsite office that takes calls, screens tenants, and provides handyman work during business hours. For smaller properties, the management team needs to have a track record managing the properties that don't have on-site services to make sure that they provide the correct oversight.

Here are a few important benefits of a good property manager:

- Provides projected financial expectations
- Compares rental rates to justify increasing rents, changing the operations, or adding value to the property
- Has the ability to operate while renovations are ongoing
- Has the ability to lower monthly fees based on more units added to their management portfolio by the active partner
- Informs owners that are looking to sell their property to other prequalified buyers
- Implements proactive marketing efforts to attract new residents
- Fulfills maintenance requests
- Provides professional management statements

Do a few minutes of online research of the property management company when reviewing a deal prior to buying in. This isn't really something that you need to take a deep dive into, but if the management company doesn't have a professional website, good reviews, and indications that they serve your target market, it may be a red flag.

- Has the active partner worked with them before?

- How long have they been in business?

- What geographic areas do they cover?

- How many units do they manage, and what is their specialization?

- How many units do they own?

- What are some of the properties nearby that they are currently managing?

Accountant (CPA)

Accountants come in many different shapes and forms. I learned the hard way when I realized that I had hired the wrong person as soon as we purchased our third property. Even though the accountant had a good track record, she didn't work with anyone doing what I was doing. Just like doctors specialize in different types of medical procedures and pilots specialize in different aircraft, accountants specialize in specific accounting practices. The accountant that the active partner uses will impact the amount of money that you keep at the end of the year when you get your two-page K-1 investor tax statement.

Real Estate, Business, and Securities Attorneys

Just like accountants, attorneys specialize in various forms of the law. Although it should be rather transparent as a passive investor, the active partner should have legal counsel in place to ensure that all the current laws are followed.

A good *real estate attorney* will ensure that the deal gets from contract to closing on time. At time of sale, a real estate attorney can make sure that all funds and contracts are being upheld.

Business attorneys will specialize in the legal documents. This attorney will generate the operating agreement and finalize the document to make sure that it follows all the updated laws and stipulations that are unique to each deal.

Securities attorneys will provide any guidance regarding the purchase or sale of equity shares. It is their job to make sure that the correct formalities and disclosures are provided.

Mortgage Broker, Banks, and Insurance Broker

A mortgage broker can be instrumental because they will be able to outsource our property to other banks prior to ownership so that we can obtain the most beneficial mortgage at purchase. Dealing direct-ly with banks can negatively impact the money we keep because we may not have a relationship with enough banks to ensure the most competitive rates and terms. The mortgage broker should have many bankers that they can market our deals to, thereby increasing the possibility of finding a lender with beneficial terms that positively impacts our bottom line.

An insurance broker can also have the same positive influence as a mortgage broker, as they should have contacts with other insurance companies. Apartment communities have different aspects that can increase or decrease the required insurance coverage; having a good insurance broker on the team ensures the correct coverage at a competitive price.

Title Agency

A title agency can create a lot of stress if they don't have a proven system and a track record of closing on time. They should be very responsive, have an eye for the fine details on the closing documents, an easy escrow process, legal expertise, and be able to comply with all regulations.

General Contractor, Subcontractors, and Handymen

Contractors, just like attorneys, specialize in different projects. The team that the general contractor employs will accelerate the project completion and save everyone time and wasted effort, as they have contacts in their industry. Renovating larger projects also lowers construction costs, as materials, appliances, and AC units can be purchased in bulk at wholesale prices.

Property Broker/Real Estate Agents/ Direct Marketing to Find Another Deal

In addition to interviewing and hiring a property manager, the active partner should be working with commercial brokers to find additional properties that haven't been listed. Off-market deals provide beneficial aspects, as they might provide seller financing, lower costs associated with the transaction, direct buyer to seller interaction, and potentially a much lower sales price.

Real estate is a 'people-heavy' business. In any one day, there are property managers, contractors, handymen, police, passersby, tenants, visitors, constables, tax collectors, active partners, and many more 'people' directly and indirectly interacting with your property to keep it operating at peak performance.

There are always outside factors with investments, but having sound processes and procedures in place greatly reduces the risk associated with apartment ownership.

CHAPTER #6

EDUCATION TO
ALLEVIATE FEAR

B efore one of my flights as a civilian student pilot, I ate a $0.78 chili dog from the gas station prior to an afternoon summer flight in Arizona. What was different then from now is that I am older, and due to my life experiences, I have certain outlooks on life that shape what I fear that are based on past experiences. Eating a chili dog and then flying in the afternoon heat of Arizona is a bad idea—you should fear this!

What I've learned after flying airplanes as a civilian and military pilot for 19 years is that the more you know, the less you fear. Even though you won't know all the answers, the more you hyperfocus, diligently practice, study, and educate yourself on a topic, the more likely you are to mitigate the risks.

You should have FEARS associated with apartment investing; that is 100% normal. Systems, processes, and proven business plans are ways to offset any unforeseen circumstances.

Following are the TOP 10 questions that I am commonly asked pertaining to passive apartment ownership and my unique way of doing business. Because our systems and processes are proprietary, there are some additional measures we take to make sure that we answer 100% of your questions prior to moving forward on the deal. Getting all of these questions answered up-front allows us to provide our customers with a well-above-average experience during every transaction.

*Please reference Appendix A for a list of additional passive investor questions.

"Dom, How Is This Different, and How Do I Know You Aren't Going to Lose My Money?"

What really takes the wind out of your sails is when you take your after-tax currency, invest it in a venture, and then lose all of it or a large portion of it to bad investment advice, a poor plan, and/or a myriad of other factors. Working in the apartment real estate industry has provided a quantifiable metric that can generate profits mathematically and systematically through our conservative underwriting process. Our current and past deals continue to operate even in the midst of the current global pandemic. Here is what we do to offset risk.

- The biggest factor that protects our deals to make sure that we don't run out of money, or overleverage ourselves, comes in the form of our established Power Team discussed in the previous chapter.

- Investor money is put into a specific property; we do not raise money with the hope that we will find a certain type of property or mix your money with other deals.

- Each investor knows what property and deal they are investing in upfront prior to committing.

- We do not count on capital appreciation, i.e., we don't buy with the hope that the property will be worth $X.XX more at a certain time in the future—that is called 'gambling.'

- We calculate an escalation in cost of operations each year in our financial projections.

- Rental income is increased at a value that is less than inflation and less than the escalating costs of running the property.

- If we plan to refinance the property, we make sure that there are several years built into the timeline to give us some flexibility in the event that lending rates have increased or if there is a market correction that would preclude us from refinancing.

- We employ a professional contracting team that specializes in apartment renovations to calculate the costs and then add an additional 10% on top of the expected cost to provide a buffer for unforeseen circumstances.

- Our accounting team uses all bank statements, profit and loss statements, and financial documents to make sure that all the money in and out of the business is tracked.

"Dom, What's in It for Me, and How Do I Know You Won't Stagnate My Investment Money?"

We provide monthly and quarterly updates and employ industry professionals for the administrative tasks: accounting, property management, construction, renovations, upgrades, and bookkeeping. The active partner's job is to oversee the property and realize which roles they can effectively fill to keep the property operating above average. Investment dollars stagnate if the power team running the project isn't researching the surrounding areas, keeping the property clean, marketing to new residents, and raising rents commensurate with or exceeding the current market trends.

During the initial portion of reviewing the business plan for a deal, make sure that the apartment community is going to meet your investment goals. Some deals are heavy-value add deals and may take 12–18 months to complete. During the renovation timeline, the property isn't making money, and there aren't going to be any cash distributions. The upside to a heavy-value add deal is that once it is rented and stabilized, the cash flow and refinancing money recaptured may be much higher. If the property is stabilized and fully leased to renters, returns could start as soon as the first quarter of ownership but may not provide as large as a payoff as a heavy-value add deal. Ultimately, you need to decide which apartment property is going to accomplish your overall wealth and income goals.

"Dom, How Do I Know This Is Real, and How Do I Know You Will Make Me Money by Diversifying in Real Estate?"

I assure you that I am a real person—you can contact me and visit me at the following website to schedule a phone call or in-person meeting:

ViperVenturesLLC.com

These are the BIG 3 things that ALL properties must do in order to make money and offset risk:

1) The property must produce cash flow.

2) The property must have a conservative fixed -rate mortgage that covers the duration of the business plan or longer.

3) The active partner in the deal must keep, monitor, and adjust adequate cash reserves in the operating account to cover the costs of running the investment, which also includes setting aside money each year for maintenance.

    a. $1,000 per unit

    b. One month's working capital

    c. $250 per unit, per year for a maintenance fund

"Dom, How Do I Start, and What Process Do You Follow That I Can Use as the Passive Investor in Each Deal?"

Please reference Chapter 4: "How passive investors participate in deals in 3 simple phases."

"Dom, Why Is This Important to Me Right Now, and When Does the Clock Start After I Transfer Funds Into the Account?"

This is important to get started now as that starts the process to actually becoming a part owner in an apartment community. The timeline for you to make money depends on each deal, but generally speaking, the equity ownership phase starts the day we legally close on the property and own the deal. Closing day starts the accounting process and is when the IRS considers your equity stake in the property effective for tax purposes. The day we own the property starts your ownership phase and the day we start making money. Every deal has its own unique details, but we generally stick to a quarterly or biannual distribution of investor profits. We can deposit money directly into your account via an ACH transfer or send you a check in the mail; whatever you would prefer.

"Dom, Why Should I Trust You, and How Much Communication Do I Expect From You?"

We provide monthly updates on properties that are undergoing renovations and that have a lot of change happening in a short period of time. At a minimum, you can expect a synopsis of your property on a quarterly basis that also shows what has been completed, property management statements, financial and bank statements, and any future planning pertaining to your project.

Every one of our properties goes into their own separate legal entity. Each legal entity that holds the property has its own separate business checking account. Every investor's contributions and cash payments are individually tracked through our accounting process. By segregating and separating all of our properties, we can keep our accounting accurate and provide quarterly updates. Additionally, our accountant can keep track of cost segregation, depreciation, cash distributions, and profit and losses throughout the year. Your taxes are easily filed accompanied by the two-page K-1 investor tax statement provided by our accounting team.

Visit the following website to view our investment properties: ViperVenturesLLC.com/projects-funded.

"Dom, How Do Your Deals Work, and How Much Do You Charge to Run the Investment? What Are Your Fees, and How Much Money Do You Invest in Each Deal?"

Generally, our investors own 70% of the equity in the property, and Viper Ventures LLC own 30% of the equity. We prioritize getting as many investors as we can in each deal that express interest. Our business plans outline how much money is required per investor and how much equity that money purchases in each deal.

The investors in the deal get all of their initial capital investment returned to them before my company earns anything. This shows that I have a massive commitment to returning your capital to you; it shows that I have a massive amount of 'skin in the game.' Additionally, once your capital is returned to you, you still hold equity in the deal, and you will receive passive cash flow commensurate with the amount of net profits received through rental income, future refinancing, or when the property is sold. My reward comes after returning all the initial capital invested in the form of equity and income from net profit, based on the equity shares owned.

Example: an investor that owns 10% equity in a deal will get all of their initial investment capital returned to them from rental income or refinancing before I make any money. Once all initial investment capital has been returned, you will receive 10% of the NET profit each year from rental income or from sale proceeds.

We do not invest in properties where we can't provide financial projections that show a return of all of our investor's initial capital contribution in less than a 10-year timeline. Using our conservative underwriting process, we calculate if the property will be able to cash-flow enough now or in the future to warrant a purchase. Our return of capital can also come through a refinance of the property to return tax-free money to our investors. The refinancing process is scrutinized to ensure that we are keeping enough reserve capital in the operating account and not mortgaging the property with more than 75% of its value.

Most, if not all, active partners in apartment deals will charge monthly, quarterly, or yearly fees, even if they do a poor job running the project. Additional fees are worked into the deal for purchase and sale.

I do not charge active partner fees.

TYPICAL DEAL MAKER FEES	0%	11.6%	11.6%
	VIPER VENTURES	OTHER INVESTOR	YOUR SAVINGS!

Viper Ventures Saves YOU TIME and MONEY
* I DON'T CHANGE FEES TO RUN THE INVESTMENT
* $0.00 IN FEES MEANS MORE MONEY INVESTED
* $0.00 IN FEES MEANS MORE MONEY BACK TO YOU

"Dom, How Do I Get Started? What's the 1st Step?"

Go to the section in this book labeled "Mission Planning Session" and follow steps 1, 2, and 3.

Visit the following website to schedule your customized Mission Planning Session call with me as your guide: ViperVenturesLLC.com/contact-us.

During this phone call, we will discuss:

- What problem do you want us to solve?

- What is important to you?

- How do you like communication sent to you?

- Do you have the income and/or assets that qualify you for the deal?

- Do you want to be the only investor in the deal, or can there be others?

- Have you ever invested in apartments before?

- What is your expectation to get all of your initial investment returned to you?

- What are your expectations on returns?

- Do you favor cash flow or an equity position higher than the other?

- What is the minimum and maximum investment timeline?

- Can you show proof of funds if we haven't worked together before?

- What amount would you like to invest?

- What timeline do I need to hit to return your initial capital contribution back to you?

- Do you prefer heavy-value add, value add, or turn-key investments? (Reference the beginning of Chapter 2 if you have questions on what each of these mean.)

- Are you willing to invest in a deal that potentially doesn't have cash flow for 1–2 years with a bigger payday later, assuming we need to do renovations?

"Dom, What Do I Have to Lose?"

As I see it, you have 3 options in front of you.

Option 1:

- Do nothing right now.

- Stay exactly where you are.

Option 2:

- Purchase a property yourself, and do everything yourself.

- Reference the Appendix and my online guides in this book to get an idea of all the big and little things required to run the deal yourself.

- Find a banker, mortgage broker, property broker, accountant, commercial insurance agent, property manager, contracting team, tax advisor, handyman, and bookkeeper to keep track of your project.

- Put together your own marketing strategy to renovate, relist, and rent out your property.

- Spend your days, nights, and weekends away from your family, wife, hobbies, and relaxing self-interests to answer phone calls from property managers, contractors, and disgruntled tenants.

Option 3:

- I'll put my proven strategies and processes to work for you.

- I'll run all the minutiae and take care of your problems the IDEAL way.

- I'll make sure your property runs great.

- I will give you more time to do the things you want to do in life.

- I will provide actual wealth that gives you cash flow so you don't run out of money before you run out of years.

"Dom, What's Going to Be Easier for Me?"

There are two types of people in the world. The first type of people dream of owning property, receiving passive income, and enjoying their lives unencumbered by problems. Another type of people act when an opportunity presents itself. Many people tell you they want to own real estate, but we both know that very few actually make it happen and even fewer own apartment communities.

It's the nature of people: the classic tale of the willful and the wishful. Most people keep dreaming, but the few who are serious about becoming a wealthy apartment owner become significantly more productive and have more fulfilling lives because they took action.

Schedule a Mission Planning Session with me today at ViperVenturesLLC.com/contact-us to get started on the profitable path to becoming a part owner of an apartment community; only you can decide.

P.S. Please reference Appendix A for a list of additional passive investor questions.

CHAPTER 7

MISSION COMMANDER
OF WEALTH

Why not do all this yourself? One word—**TIME.** Ideas are being challenged at our core levels across our nation. Teachers give gold stars to everyone in their class regardless of merit, effort exerted, or actual achievement. High school graduates that attend college to build a future for themselves are getting riddled with soul-crushing college debt. As I write this book, U.S. college debt is $1,590,000,000,000. That's $1.59 trillion. 1.59 million times 1 million.

Even worse, universities are largely indoctrinating unprofitable economic philosophies as the go-to and acceptable way of doing business. This is happening in such a significant number of the younger population that they are starting to view these ways of living as a positive way to normalize and make their status rise because we will all be treated the same.

Worse yet, there is an erroneous idea that everything should be free. When someone doesn't pay anything for something, it waters down, dilutes, and ultimately makes that item worth nothing. Eventually, nontechnical college degrees will be worth absolutely nothing. We will see a sharp rise in the right-brained individuals in the next 20 years that are going to make the lion's share of the profit. Pilots, doctors, lawyers, and technical professions will make a great living, but the creative thinkers that take a nontraditional approach to wealth stand to gain the most, even if it is within the aforementioned industries.

There will still be people that attend college for a technical degree, but the real money to be made will be in nontraditional forms. Fortunately, there are other methods to profit from this demographic shift—apartment community ownership is a nontraditional approach to Proactive Wealth.

Questions to ask before doing this yourself:

- Are you fully committed to putting the entire cost of the down payment towards the mortgage?

- How much additional capital will you need in the future?

- Does the property you are purchasing need repairs?

- Do you have a solid grasp of what repairs are going to cost?

- What type of tenant does the neighborhood command?

- What type of asset and piece of real estate is going to work for you in a given market?

- Are you willing to be a landlord?

- Do you know all the legal ramifications of being a landlord?

- Do you know that the law generally protects the 'little-guy' that will be living in your property and potentially abusing it?

- Are you willing to fork over the several thousand dollars in eviction fees, repairs, turnover costs, and time that it takes when managing a property?

- Are you willing to stomach the disgust you get from another property owner that puts their car on blocks, doesn't upkeep their front yard, and plays loud music, thereby degrading the amount of money you could charge when renting out your place?

- How well do you know the city that you are considering?

- Do you know that all real estate is very local and can change year by year?

- Do you know that properties less than five units have a value driven by the local real estate and not the rents they collect?

Are you a 'hands-on, I must control every aspect of the deal' kind of person? Or rather, are you the type of person that is willing to spend the time to learn some of the industry's information and then subsequently place your money into a deal that is run for you, thereby saving you a lot of time? Smaller real estate deals are definitely manageable by even average humanoids like myself, but if you really want to see your wealth grown proactively, apartments are the way to go. When I purchased the first apartment, I was already in over my head trying to do it all by myself.

I didn't have the time to interview tenants, deal with evictions, fix toilets and sinks, oversee renovations, conduct accounting, produce effective marketing, pay the bills and taxes, and complete all the administrative tasks that must go on each month. I had to triage and outsource much of these tasks to industry professionals, hence the Power Team. My ability to accelerate the business plans on multiple properties was strongly driven by the power team of market and industry professionals that I assembled to help me on a per-job basis with our projects.

Hire Slow—Fire Fast

During the first year in business, I had to replace 75 percent of the people that I initially hired. Some of the people on the team that I fired really hurt; my bookkeeper, tax advisor, contractor and accountant were all difficult to replace but necessary for growth. Having the right people, doing the right task, is important to generate predictable profits.

If you have read this far, you are most likely someone who likes to see forward momentum and someone who values growth and prosperity. Do you measure your success by the accumulation of currency? We have all seen or heard of individuals that have lots of money but are still failures in life. Too many of the rich are still failures, and too many poor have mastered the art of living but don't have any money to show for it.

The measure is not how much a man gets but rather how he plans to use it for others. True living is contentment, joy, usefulness, and growth through your given talents.

Be—Do—Have

I had this out of order for a long time in my life and put the "doing" portion first. This led me to into a very active day that didn't produce results, and I didn't ever really "have" what I was looking to achieve. Once I prioritized being a different person, the doing portion of the equation made much more sense and generated a far better result.

Be Honest

For things to get better, I needed to be better. I am presenting this information to you because I feel like it would be an injustice for you to go into your later years not knowing the amount of financial stability and wealth that you stand to gain by investing in apartment communities. My enthusiasm coupled with action and ability has generated new opportunities for investors, family, charitable organizations, and myself.

Is money the root of all evil or is the love of money the root of all evil?

Clinging to your past experiences that have been riddled with poor outcomes may be your limiting belief that you need to overcome. Your know-how is strongly influenced by your doing mindset. The what and how is not as important as the inspiration to action. Action produces genius, magic, and power. When you decide to take action, the atoms in your brain vibrate at a powerful level that produces results and otherwise unexplainable "coincidences" happening in your life.

Conduct research and be educated, but don't cripple your ability to make a decision with so much figuring. If you are sitting around figuring all the time or waiting for everything to be just right before taking action, you're likely to wait your entire life. Take more swings at pitches that aren't perfect, and get your share of singles and doubles every day. *Heroes* exert a considerable amount of control over their own destiny through action.

The hero in our story is the passive investor: you. God put us on this earth to live the largest life possible and to help others do the same. That *large life* is attainable by passively investing in *apartments*.

CHAPTER 8

THE LOST CHAPTER— A SPOUSE'S PERSPECTIVE

This chapter provides a different prospective for your significant other or investing partner. My wife, Danielle, provided some insight on how she views what we are doing. This section isn't aimed at trying to convince you to do anything you don't want to do, rather it is an attempt to provide a little background on this passive investment vehicle through the 'eyes' of another that isn't involved in every aspect of the business.

Please visit ViperVenturesLLC.com/resources for a completely FREE download of "The Lost Chapter— A Spouse's Perspective."

We don't ask for any contact info—this is completely FREE, and you won't be spammed by reading this chapter specifically designed for this book.

If you have additional questions, concerns or feedback, contact me at: ViperVenturesLLC.com/contact-us.

CHAPTER 9

THE NEXT STEP

Now, you get to make the decision. You've heard my reasons. I'm not in this business for a quick turn-and-burn. I'm in this for the relationships that will be fostered, the lives that will be changed, the properties that we will all get to fix, the money that we will all save and reinvest, and the long-term growth that will come from solid consistency that is provided by apartments.

You can be part of a complex system that allows investors to hold equity in tangible property that generates above-average returns. If you, like me, have made poor investments in the past, this one is not one of those decisions. Rest assured, I will never abuse my investors for a short-term profit. I look forward to making you more than a million dollars in apartment investments and much more.

Would you be interested to know that there are 100% anti-traditional investing platforms that have proven strategies that are currently helping civilian pilots, military pilots, and working-class professionals?

Time, freedom, convenience, ease, cash flow, Proactive Wealth. You can have it all.

P.S. Make sure to ask about our exclusive Single Seat Millionaire Equity Club.

WHAT TO DO NEXT?

1) Visit ViperVenturesLLC.com/contact-us.

2) Enter your info and send me a message.

3) I'll reach out to you and schedule a personal call with me at a time that works for you.

This short phone call with me will be a quick data -gathering conversation to see if I could help you with any pain points in your life and to see what type of strategy you are looking to achieve. Our call together will help define what you think you would like to do if we decide to work together and to see if we would be a good fit.

Be certain, this is a two-way interview to make sure we are a good match for each other. Real estate is a methodical process coupled with a long-term relationship, so we need to make sure we are on the same page. Let's get it correct the first time.

Schedule a custom Mission Planning Session with me now to get started on the profitable path of being a passive apartment investor. Only you can decide.

Visit ViperVenturesLLC.com/contact-us.

Thank you for your valuable time and consideration. I look forward to talking with you.

P.S. Make sure to ask about our exclusive Single Seat Millionaire Equity Club.

ADDITIONAL INVESTOR QUESTIONS

"Dom, Show Me a Proven Passive & Hands-Off Approach to Invest in Real Estate."

This is easier to demonstrate if the active partner has already done some deals and has experience in the local market. The business plan will show the financial viability behind the deal but just as important to the numbers is the ability of the active partner to close the deal and run the plan with operational efficiency. Even though you won't be actively running the day-to-day operations on the apartment investment, it is important that you understand or at least grasp a few of the concepts that go on behind the scenes so you can be armed with the necessary data to oversee your investment and ask the right questions. You need to understand how the deal is structured and how all the members on the power team participate.

"Dom, How Do I Know Who Is on the Power Team for Your Deals?"

All of our business plans include a section at the end that outlines the profiles, businesses, and professionals that are directly impacting our bottom line. Chapter 5 in this book defines who should be on an active partner's power team.

"Dom, How Many Other Investors Will Be in on the Deal?"

Every deal is placed in its own legal entity and therefore has the capability to have only one investor and myself in the deal if we structure it that way. If you choose to be the only investor in the deal, you will have to put a much larger capital contribution towards the down payment, acquisition cost, cash reserves, and any planned renovations that need to occur in the business plan. Unless an investor is adamant about being the only one in the deal, we try our hardest to get everyone that has interest in the deal to partake so that they can accelerate their wealth accumulation. In the event that an investor doesn't have the capital lined up in time, we place them at the top of the list for the next purchase and acquisition project.

"Dom, How Do I Know How to File My Taxes at the End of the Year?"

Each property is registered and owned by its own unique legal entity. Each entity is taxed as a partnership by the IRS because there is more than one investor on each deal. Because we segregate all of our properties, we are able to provide an accurate K-1 tax statement to each investor prior to tax time each year. This 2-page document usually shows a net loss on paper allowing you to protect the income earned through the property due to the legal tax benefits afforded to apartment communities. If you invested in a deal and didn't own equity in the project but received cash distributions, our accountant will provide a 1099-INT statement that is very similar to one you received from your bank account or stock trades.

"Dom, Can I Use Funds From My IRA or 401 (K) to Invest in One of Your Deals?"

The short answer is yes.

It may come as no surprise, but many shy away from using their IRA in an apartment community because it seems complicated; it's not. Your money that you have sitting in those funds is 100% legal to move into a passive apartment community and also has the blessing from the IRS to be invested and tax deferred! While you can't invest in real estate directly through an employer-sponsored 401(k), you can choose to roll a former employer's 401(k) account into an individual retirement account (IRA). Prior to moving funds into a new account, check to see if the current account already allows you to "self-direct" the funds to invest in real estate; if no, then all you have to do is simply move the money into an account that gives you the control to invest in real estate. IRA and 401(k) managers aren't going to tell you that you can self-direct your money because then they don't get their fees. That nasty "F" word; FEES.

Here are the basic steps to using an IRA or 401(k) to passively invest:

- Check your IRA or 401(k) account and see if it allows you to "self-direct" the funds.

- If yes, then talk with a representative about the process.

- If no, locate a self-directed custodian and move funds into the new account (setting up the new account and moving funds takes about 2-weeks).

- Once your funds have registered in your new account, look for a deal to invest in and ask your custodian what paperwork is required once you invest to let the active partner know.

- Find a deal and send the custodian for your account the required paperwork.

- When the deal is closed, you will now own a passive investment that has an income stream that is tax deferred!

"Dom, What Do I Do If I Need to Sell My Position and Get out of the Deal?"

Real estate is an illiquid asset and I advise upfront prior to getting into a deal that investors should be willing to keep their money in the deal for ten years. This is more of a mindset versus a hard and fast rule. Every project has a separate operating agreement that outlines expectations and is specific to each property purchased. Contained within the operating agreement, you will find the value of your equitable position and what to do in the event you need to cash out of the project.

We forecast our financial projections out to 10-years in our business plans but would always consider selling sooner if we received an offer that was too good to pass up. Conversely, if we experience a market correction during the timeline that we would like to sell, we hold on to the property until the market comes back to achieve a better return. The disposition of the property isn't set in stone. The viability of selling is always weighed on the current market and to achieve the maximum amount of money.

"Dom, What Happens During a Global Pandemic or During a Market Crash?"

This really depends, as I have only read about the crash of 1929 and subsequent crashes throughout history. The market corrections that I have personally been a part of have been the housing crash of 2008–2009 and the corona virus of 2019–2020. Both of these market crashes have some specific distinctions that are noteworthy. Due to the housing market crash of 2008, many were forced from their homes and moved into rental properties. Many apartment owners not only collected income, but also raised rents during this time due to the demand for affordable living.

During the corona virus of 2019, many service industry tenants were forced out of a job or were required to stay home. Even though some rents came in late, we were still able to hold our properties, pay our mortgages and bills, and keep tenants in place.

"Dom, How Much Net Worth or Income Do I Need to Have to Legally Invest?"

The active partner will have investment criteria that their investors must meet. Most require a NET worth of $1 million+, not including your own residence, or $200,000+ annual income with the expectation that you will make that income for the next 2+

years. These are securities guidelines, but there are other legal ways to still invest if you don't meet these restrictions.

"Dom, What Should I Look for In the Legal Documents?"

For each property, there is a separate and unique legal operating agreement that outlines the following (this list is not all inclusive but a good guide to what should be considered):

- Investor shares and equity percentage owned
- Articles of the organization
- Capital account rules & contribution stipulations
- Changes in control of the legal entity
- Company's method of accounting
- Stipulations for a deceased member, deceased spouse, or divorce
- Distribution expectations
- Rules for disposition and sale
- Economic risk of loss
- Event of dissolution & dissociation
- Initial capital contributions of members and managers
- What a 'majority' vote means

- Duties and expectations of the active members running the project
- Outline of the debt rules and restrictions
- Membership interests (money, net losses, net profits, notices)
- Organization expenses and expectations
- Permitted & authorized transfer of ownership
- Legal definition of the subject property
- Special majority voting rules
- Federal income tax treatment
- Acts requiring special or unanimous vote of members
- Limitation of liability of the manager (i.e., active partner)
- Stipulation on the use of the property's bank accounts
- Appointment rules of a new manager
- Manager's conflicts of interest & rules for compensation
- Fiduciary duties of the manager
- Meetings of members
- Priority and return of capital contributions
- Books of account and records
- Member's capital account

- Loans
- Restrictions of transferability, withdrawal, and permitted transfers
- Right of first refusal
- Buy/sell options
- Voluntary purchase options
- Conflict of provisions
- Purchase price, terms, limitations on payments
- Dissociation of a member
- Rights of assignees, substitute members, additional members
- Dissolution and liquidation of assets
- Articles of termination
- Amendment or modification of Operating Agreement
- Attorney fees and laws
- Dispute resolution
- Heirs, successors and assigns
- Notices and references
- Representation by counsel
- Rights of creditors and third parties under the agreement
- Time periods and waivers

"Dom, How Do I Study the Real Estate Market to Educate Myself?"

What do you look for in a deal being that real estate markets are so local?

How do you select a target investment market?

Once you select your target market, do you know enough about the city, submarket, neighborhood, and street?

The widely accepted idea that location, location, location, is all you need when it comes to multi-family real estate investing is WRONG. Our properties have generated profitable returns by investing in the direction of growth. That property may not look enticing because of the surrounding neighborhood, but if there are jobs, growth, colleges, schools, and there is a positive demographic shift, you may be in for a pleasant surprise.

A nice property in a nice location doesn't make a whole lot of money if not overseen correctly, purchased for too much, or poorly operated and maintained. Conversely, a property in an up-and-coming area that is renovated and well-kept may provide a much better rate of return on your investment coupled with efficient operations, city, job, and population growth.

Selecting the target market is only one of the many considerations when investing in multi-family real estate. There are specific geographical areas that I have chosen to avoid because even though I know that the cash returns may be higher, the work and risk associated with those areas does not outweigh the prospective gains. We choose submarkets within the city based on the city's plans to develop and generate future growth, other investor's moving into a market, more development, businesses moving in, demographic shifts, and population growth.

You cannot pick the "perfect" market, but using some of these principles, you will arm yourself with the data used to start your search. When you are starting out and trying to pick what markets to invest in, consider these resources for evaluation:

- US city data www.usa.com/

- Census ("Demographic and Housing Estimates") www.census.gov/

- Integra Realty Resources (IRR)—Annual Viewpoint www.irr.com/research

- CBRE Biannual Cap Rate Survey www.cbre.us/research-and-reports/North-America-Cap-Rate-Survey

- Marcus & Millichap Annual US Multifamily Investment Forecast www.marcusmillichap.com/research/researchreports

- Zillow Annual Consumer House Trends Reports www.zillow.com/research/zillow-group -report-2016-13279/

- US Bureau of Labor Statistics www.bls.gov/

- Rich Blocks Poor Blocks www.richblockspoorblocks.com/

- Milken Institute www..milkeninstitute.org/ explore/research-and-analysis

- Best Places to Live www.bestplaces.net/

- National Multifamily Housing Council www.nmhc.org/

- American Apartment Owners Association www.american-apartment-owners-association.org/

You can use the websites above to answer the following questions below:

Is the population expanding or contracting?

- Calculate the growth in the Metropolitan Statistical Area (MSA).

- Calculate the population growth in the submarket of the city.

- For MSA data—"Annual Estimate of the Resident Population" Census.gov.

- For city data—"Annual Population Estimates" Census.gov.

Demographic age?

- "Demographic and Housing Estimates" Census.gov.

- Compare the increase or decrease in age to the asset you are considering.

- A younger population may favor affordable housing.

- A mid-aged population may consider luxury apartments.

- An older demographic age puts assisted living facilities in demand.

Unemployment?

- "Selected Economic Characteristics" data table on the Census.gov website

- Consider 1, 3, 5, & 10-year trends.

- Trending upward or downward?

Major employers—Job and business growth?

- "Selected Economic Characteristics" Census.gov

- Check to make sure that any 1 employer doesn't control more than 25% of the employment in the area.

- Who are the top employers in the area?

- Search for "city name + top employers" on Google.

- Are businesses moving into the area?

Supply and Demand (vacancy rates on 5+ unit multifamily buildings)?

- Reference Census.gov "Selected Housing Characteristics" for vacancy rates.

- What is the current vacancy rate in the past 5 years?

- The MSA annual construction page on Census.gov can give you an idea if the building permits are going up, which potentially means fewer vacancies.

- If you are in an area that has an increasing population and strong employers, the rents collected should be increased to at least match inflation on a year-to-year basis.

All of this fact finding is good but only a piece of what is required to get the deal done. Every deal has its own challenges, its unforeseen problems, and its upsides that lead to profit. Beware of getting so inundated with the minutiae that it prevents you from taking the next step. We live in an imperfect world; analyzing things to perfection may lead to paralysis.

If you have any questions on the data contained in this chapter or any questions at all in your search, please contact me.

ABOUT
DOMINIC "SLICE" TEICH

8 14 knots—canopy melting speed. That's not near-
ly as fast as Dominic Teich is flying through his
civilian and military flying career as a decorated F-16
instructor pilot, which included 69 combat missions
and 2 deployments to Iraq, Syria, and Afghanistan.
To fly a fighter jet, you have to have a plan; to purchase apartments for PROFIT, you need a PLAN.

By the age of 18, Dominic was teaching civilian
pilots and only 4 years later was instructing Air Force
pilots chosen for the Fighter Track. He currently in-
structs fighter pilots in the F-16 school house at Luke
AFB, AZ, and runs a full-time apartment investing
company.

Dominic is a sought-out instructor. He started out
teaching high school math, downhill skiing, music,
and civilian aviation and is now a graduated and dec-

orated F-16 instructor pilot. No good fighter pilot takes off with their fingers crossed; that's not how to deal with risk. Dominic brings his instructor background, his tactical, aggressive, and problem-solving mindset, that has been honed over many years as a fighter pilot, to apartment investing. And he considers this his true single-seat method to help passive investors increase profit, decrease their tax burden, provide equity, generate cash flow, and ultimately provide life-long Proactive Wealth accumulation.

Even after two combat tours in the Middle East, Dominic continues to teach in the 69th Fighter Squadron at Luke AFB as an F-16 instructor pilot and has grown an apartment business to share these opportunities with others. He is a husband, father, fighter pilot, author, businessman, and leader. All of this has been accomplished with only a slightly average IQ and an unending desire to WIN and PROFIT.

Dominic is married to his best friend Danielle of 10 years. Danielle's insights and contributions to the business have been an invaluable source of inspiration. Her guidance, forethought, and outside views have indirectly, directly, and profitably helped the continued growth of the family and business. As vice president of Viper Ventures LLC, she is the most important person on the team because she brings such a valuable perspective. Dominic is the proud father of three beautiful children: Isla, Max, and Anna. All three children started their passive investing careers in apartments and know how important it is to proactively grow their wealth.

When he's not raging around on fire in his fighter jet, you can find him on his properties, camping with his son, mountain biking, or spending time with his wife and kids on the beach. Dominic was recently voted as "World's Best Dad" by 2/3 of his children.

Sweet Anna was named after Anna Schindler, our cousin that died from cancer just after turning seven years old and has been such a great inspiration for our business, giving, and helping others. (The Anna Schindler Cancer Foundation is a lean organization that efficiently and effectively directs over 93% of your contributions to families in need. AnnaSchindlerFoundation.org).

To learn more about Dominic's past projects and future opportunities, visit: ViperVenturesLLC.com/projects-funded.

If you are looking for unique opportunities that generate Proactive Wealth through apartments coupled with above average experiences for your life, contact Dominic at ViperVenturesLLC.com/contact-us.

AUTHOR RESOURCES

We offer some additional FREE resources via our website that can help you.

The Wealth Tracker

- This spreadsheet is an easy way to track your personal equity you own in real estate.

- Easily input your data to track your net worth & wealth.

- *Note: if you are already a world-class passive investor of Viper Ventures LLC, I will fill this out for you.

We will be making more resources as time goes on that are short, informative, and helpful to track your progress to financial freedom.

Please visit ViperVenturesLLC.com/resources to claim a free copy of the Wealth Tracker.

P.S. don't forget to ask about the Single Seat Millionaire Equity Club.

SCAN the following code with your smart phone to get to the resources page on the Viper Ventures website:

NOTES

Download Your Bonus Gifts!

You have taken time out of your busy day and will be rewarded with a FREE gift! I created a simple must-have gift for you located on the front page of our website.

- YOU won't be spammed.

- Your data will not be sold to any 3rd parties.

- This is a valuable report that answers the top 20 questions of passive apartment investing.

- The only exchange is your name and email.

- This FREE report will answer questions and is easily viewable on your smart phone by scanning the following code or viewed by entering ViperVenturesLLC.com into a web browser.

Made in the USA
San Bernardino, CA
20 June 2020